WHEN ALL YOU DO IS CRY

WHEN ALL YOU DO IS CRY

WENDY HOOD

CHAPTERS

PART IV: After the Storm

INTRODUCTION

There are times when you cry, and you don't even know why. The tears arrive quietly, uninvited but familiar. They fall while you're washing dishes, or in the stillness after a conversation that didn't touch what truly needed to be said. Sometimes they spill while you're listening to a song that doesn't even match your mood—or maybe it does, but only your soul knows how.

Crying, they say, is weakness. But that's a lie told by those who were never given space to feel.

This flood wasn't just water. It wasn't simple sadness. It was grief layered over confusion, layered over disappointment, layered over exhaustion—sealed tightly by years of being strong because there was no other option. Your strength didn't stop the tide. It only delayed it. And now, here it is, not asking for permission.

You weren't crying because of one thing. You were crying because of *everything*.

The day your heart first broke and no one noticed.
The time you forgave and got hurt again.
The moment you said "I'm fine" and no one asked again.
The night you didn't sleep, the smile you faked, the support you gave while running on empty.

And it all collected—emotion after emotion, year after year—until your body did what your mouth could not. It spoke the ancient language of water.

The language of overflow.
The language of release.

Crying is not your enemy. It is your healer, your storyteller, your backup voice when the weight of your silence gets too loud. Every tear is an acknowledgment of what was buried. And with each drop, something rises—truth, clarity, permission, or maybe even peace.

So no, this flood wasn't just water. It was history. It was healing. It was the soul making room to breathe again.

1

The Cry That Comes
Without Warning

There's a cry that sneaks up on you. It doesn't wait for an event, a breakup, a funeral, or a fight. It doesn't politely announce its arrival. It just... erupts. Sometimes gently, like a quiet tremor behind the eyes. Other times violently, like a storm ripping through your chest. And you're left wondering, *What just broke inside me?* But the truth is—it wasn't sudden. It was building.

Your body always knows before your mind does.

The cry that comes without warning is often a whisper from your nervous system that something has been *too much for too long*. It doesn't need permission from your logic or your schedule. It doesn't care that you're at work or in the middle of a task. It will show up in a meeting, on the train, or while folding laundry—and you'll feel the lump rise in your throat like it's always been there, waiting.

You try to blink it away. Hold your breath. Clench your jaw. Swallow it down like every other emotion you've been told is "too much." But eventually, the leak becomes a flood. Because what you never said is still alive in you. What you never processed is still circling your chest like it's looking for an exit. And this kind of cry is the body's way of opening that exit when you've refused to.

Sometimes it's not about sadness. It's about *finally feeling.*

It could be years of abandonment echoing from childhood.

Or the disappointment you normalized so well, you forgot it hurt.

Or the weight of responsibility you've carried without applause.

Or simply a buildup of days where you've smiled when you needed rest.

Whatever the source, your body has a threshold. And when your words can't carry the load, your tears do. They come with no explanation because the explanation is too layered, too nuanced, too old, or too deep to summarize. But your body doesn't need a summary. It just knows it's time.

So let them fall.

You don't have to understand the cry to honor it.

You don't have to explain it to justify it.

You just have to let it speak.

Because the cry that comes without warning is never really random. It's ancient. It's intelligent. And it's trying to tell you that *you matter enough* to stop pretending nothing hurts.

2

Held Too Long

Some people learn early how to cry.
Others learn how not to.

You may have been taught—directly or indirectly—that your emotions made others uncomfortable. That your sadness was inconvenient. That your anger was "too much." That your voice, especially when trembling, was a liability instead of a truth.

So you learned to hold it in.
To smile when you were aching.
To say "I'm okay" with tears burning behind your eyes.
To breathe through pain like it was just another daily task.

But what happens when you hold something in for too long?
It starts to live inside of you.
Held grief doesn't disappear—it morphs into exhaustion.
Held rage doesn't resolve—it simmers into resentment.
Held sorrow doesn't dissolve—it shapes itself into silence, into numbness, into self-doubt.

Emotional bottling is the art of pretending. And suppression is the heavy cost of survival when safety isn't an option. When you've had to perform strength just to be respected, loved, or left alone. You bottle because showing everything feels dangerous. You suppress because falling apart seems like a luxury you can't afford.

But what you suppress eventually spills. And not always in tears.

Sometimes it shows up as anxiety in rooms that feel too crowded. Sometimes it's a short temper you can't explain.

Sometimes it's forgetfulness, fatigue, migraines, or a body that constantly aches with no medical cause.

Sometimes it's a constant need to help others, so you don't have to sit with your own unmet needs.

And too often, it's a life where you don't feel *fully here*—just functioning.

Survival mode does not mean you're thriving. It means you're enduring. And endurance is a sacred thing—but it is not meant to be your permanent home.

What happens when emotions are held too long?

You forget how to let go.

You forget how to ask for help.

You begin to fear your own softness.

You equate feeling with failing.

But the truth is: those bottled tears still want to be cried. Those silenced emotions still want to be heard. And no amount of pretending can make your spirit forget what it needs.

So maybe this chapter is not about crying at all.

Maybe it's about *permission*.

To feel without shame.

To express without punishment.

To live without always holding something back.

Because everything you've held too long has been holding *you* in return.

It's time to release it.

3

The Invisible Pain

There is a kind of pain that doesn't scream.

It doesn't leave visible bruises, doesn't break bones, doesn't draw attention.

It's dressed in well-put-together outfits. It keeps appointments. It texts back with hearts and exclamation points.

It laughs when it needs to. It shows up on time. It remembers birthdays.

This pain hides in plain sight.

Because it's learned to.

The invisible pain is the ache you carry in silence—because saying "I'm not okay" never brought relief before. It's the kind of sadness that has learned how to look like competence, how to smile so convincingly it convinces *you*, too. How to stay quiet, even when something inside is begging to be known.

You're praised for being strong. But strength has become your disguise.

Because if people knew the truth—the emptiness, the tears you've cried into your pillow, the way you sometimes wish life would just *pause*—they wouldn't know what to do with it. They'd try to fix you. Or worse, avoid you.

So you silence it. You say, "I'm tired."

But what you really mean is: *I feel alone in a way I can't even explain.*

Invisible pain shows up as chronic tension in your body.

As fake laughs that drain you instead of lift you.

As forgetting how long it's been since you truly rested—not just your body, but your soul.

You've trained yourself to be okay enough to not worry anyone. But what about you?

What about the version of you who cries behind locked doors?

What about the one who doesn't know how to ask for affection without feeling needy?

What about the strength that feels more like a prison than a virtue?

Sometimes we wear our sadness like armor.

We smile because it's safer than unraveling.

We stay silent because we've been misunderstood too many times before.

But pain doesn't disappear just because it's hidden well. It waits. It speaks through your body, your dreams, your misaligned choices, your fatigue. And eventually, it demands to be witnessed.

Invisible pain needs visibility—not necessarily from others, but from *you.*

So today, acknowledge what you've been hiding behind your strength.

Say it softly: *I'm carrying more than they know.*

And then remind yourself: *Even if no one sees it, it's real. And it matters.*

Because invisible doesn't mean imagined.

It means *unseen.*

And it deserves your light.

4

People Don't Ask Why

You'd think that tears would draw compassion.

That a trembling voice or a swollen eye would trigger concern, curiosity, or at the very least... presence.

But often, it doesn't.

Instead, people freeze.

They look away.

They pretend they didn't see.

Or worse, they make a joke, change the subject, or excuse themselves with a well-timed phone call.

And you're left sitting there—wet cheeks, clenched jaw, holding back the flood with your own trembling hands—feeling like your pain made *them* uncomfortable.

Why don't they ask?

Maybe because they don't know what to do with truth.

Maybe because they were raised to fear emotions, to suppress vulnerability, to walk past pain like it's a stranger on the street.

Maybe because asking "Why are you crying?" opens the door to things they're not ready to hear... or feel.

And maybe, just maybe, some of them never learned to care past convenience.

The truth is, when you cry in front of people, you're revealing something sacred. Something raw. Something honest. You're offering a moment where masks fall, where roles pause, where the soul speaks. But not everyone is built to listen. Not everyone is safe enough to hold that kind of truth. And some don't want the responsibility of seeing you clearly.

So instead, they look at your tears like they're not human. Like you're a glitch in the script.

And in that moment, you begin to wonder: *Am I too much?*

No.

You are not too much.

They're just too far removed from their own softness to meet you in yours.

And still—it hurts.

To be seen but not *asked*.

To cry and have no one reach.

To be surrounded, yet alone in your unraveling.

It creates a wound deeper than the sadness itself: *the wound of emotional abandonment in real time.*

But you can stop internalizing their distance.

You can stop shrinking your truth just to make others more comfortable.

Your tears don't require permission.

They don't need validation.

They don't need applause.

They just need space—and sometimes, silence.

And if no one asks you why, ask *yourself*.

Gently. Kindly.

Why am I crying right now?

What part of me is asking to be held, seen, understood, released?

Because even if they don't ask, you can.

And that is where the healing begins.

5

The Isolation Inside The Ache

There's a kind of loneliness that doesn't come from being alone.

It comes from being surrounded—but *unfelt*.

From trying to explain your sadness to people who can only nod politely.

From reaching for comfort and grabbing air.

This kind of ache is quiet, but it's deep.

It doesn't just hurt—you feel *lost* inside of it.

Not because you don't know who you are, but because no one else seems to see you clearly.

You speak in full sentences and still feel unheard.

You show up to the conversation and still feel invisible.

You weep, hoping someone will lean in, and they do... but only with surface questions, only with platitudes, only enough to say they tried.

And then you're left holding the rawness alone.

That's what this chapter is about.

Not just crying, but crying *through* the realization that you may be living a life where your deepest feelings are your most private truths—shared only with the ceiling, the pillow, or the late-night silence.

The isolation doesn't come just from the pain. It comes from the *disconnect*.

You start to feel like an island. Like everyone else is living light and linear, while you're moving through emotional oceans without a map. You start to feel like maybe something is wrong with you—because no one seems to *get it*, and you've grown tired of trying to explain.

That exhaustion? That's grief too.

Not the grief of losing someone, but the grief of feeling emotionally unmatched, emotionally misplaced, emotionally *alone*.

And that kind of grief settles into your bones. It makes you retreat. It makes you quiet. It makes you stop reaching, because what's the point in trying if the echo's the only one answering back?

But even in that echo... is you.

You, reflecting back your truth.

You, honoring your depth, even if no one else does.

You, refusing to go numb just because others have.

The ache of not being understood will tempt you to silence yourself. But don't.

Because somewhere, someone knows this feeling too.

And because *you* understanding you may be the most sacred thing of all.

It's okay to need someone to get it.

It's also okay to be the first one who truly *does*.

6

❧

Every Tear Has A Memory

Not all tears come from the present.
Some come from years ago.
From moments your mind had to forget just to keep you moving.
From experiences you minimized, buried, or tried to rationalize because they didn't seem "big enough" to break you.

But your body never forgot.
Your soul recorded it all.

The sound of disappointment.
The feeling of being overlooked.
The night you cried as a child and no one came.
The first time someone said they loved you, then used that love to control or hurt you.
The thousand tiny betrayals that added up to a mountain of silence.

You may not remember the dates.
You may not recall the details.
But your tears *know*.
They rise when a familiar energy returns.
When a situation smells, sounds, or feels like the past—even if your conscious mind can't put a name to it.

This is your body doing sacred work.

It's remembering the unspeakable, the unprocessed, the tucked-away grief that never got to stretch its legs and speak its truth.

Every tear carries data.

A story. A name. A feeling that once had nowhere to go.

And now that it finally has a way out, it travels through your tear ducts—like little memory messengers finally being released.

That's why crying can feel so overwhelming.

Because it's not always about what's happening *now*.

It's about what *has happened*—and how long it's been trapped inside.

Maybe the tears come because you were strong for too long.

Maybe they come because something minor today reminded your body of something major back then.

Maybe they come because the version of you who couldn't cry at the time... finally feels safe enough to do it now.

And that's not weakness. That's healing.

That's restoration.

That's time collapsing in on itself to offer you another chance to feel what you were never allowed to before.

So when the tears come, don't rush to wipe them.

Don't shame them.

Don't silence them with distraction.

Ask:

Whose tears are these?

What are they trying to free me from?

What memory are they washing clean?

Because every tear has a memory.

And every memory finally honored... becomes lighter.

7

Tears As Prayer

There are times when words fail.

When your voice trembles too much to speak.

When you can't form the sentence, can't finish the thought, can't explain what's unraveling inside of you.

But the tears come.

And that *is* the prayer.

Crying is a sacred language. One that the Divine understands perfectly. There are no grammar rules, no need for clarity, no need to pretend you're okay. Just release. Just truth. Just presence. And sometimes, that is the most honest conversation you'll ever have with God.

You don't need a pulpit to pray.

You don't need a robe, a scripture, or a song.

Sometimes all you need is the sound of your own soul cracking open.

Tears are not just emotional—they're spiritual.

They carry surrender.

They carry the weight of what you can no longer carry.

They say what your lips don't know how to shape: *Help me. Heal me. Hold me. I don't know what else to do.*

That is prayer.

Every drop is a wordless plea.

A confession.

A letting go.

A petition written in salt water.

Some tears come when you're grieving. Others come when you're overwhelmed. But some tears come when you *feel* something so pure—love, mercy, release—that you can't contain it. Those are the tears of reverence. The tears of encounter. The tears that show you that even in your breaking, you are being met.

Sometimes when you cry, you're not weeping *alone*—you're interceding.

Not just for yourself, but for your mother, your ancestors, your child, your community, even strangers who have never learned to cry for themselves.

Tears can be that holy. That powerful. That connected.

And when you feel something shift after crying... that wasn't just your nervous system calming down. That was heaven responding. That was the energy clearing. That was your inner altar releasing a burden it was never meant to hold alone.

So don't downplay your tears.

Don't apologize for the puddle they leave.

Don't feel ashamed if all you can offer God some days is the water running down your face.

Because in that offering—raw, wordless, trembling—is intimacy.

And God listens most intently to the prayers we don't know how to speak.

8

⚜

Grief In Disguise

S ometimes you think you're just having a rough day.
You're emotional, on edge, teary for no clear reason.
But if you slow down and listen deeper, you'll realize: this isn't just sadness.

It's *grief*—but wearing another face.

Grief doesn't always enter the room holding a funeral program.

Sometimes it shows up dressed as irritation.

Sometimes it wears numbness, or fatigue, or that empty feeling you can't quite name.

Sometimes it looks like procrastination or feeling disconnected from yourself.

Sometimes it's hiding beneath your strength, waving from behind your "I'm fine."

And what's grieving might not be a person.

It might be a version of you that no longer fits.

A role you've outgrown.

A dream that didn't happen.

A relationship that shifted before you were ready.

Or the realization that you're not who you used to be—and you don't fully recognize who you're becoming either.

That's *identity death*. And it hurts.

You may not have had a ceremony for it, but your soul did.

Your spirit noticed the shift.

It marked the moment when innocence was lost, when safety was compromised, when the self you once knew faded into memory.

And now your body weeps—not just for the loss, but for the confusion.

Because transitions, even the good ones, carry grief.

When something ends—whether it's a season, a relationship, a chapter, or a role—you lose more than the thing itself.

You lose the comfort of knowing who you were in relation to it.

You lose the routine, the meaning, the mirrored identity.

And no one talks about that enough.

No one warns you that even healing will require grieving.

That growth costs you the version of you that survived, coped, adapted, endured.

Grief in disguise is hard to treat because it doesn't ask for obvious comfort. It just sits in you—subtle, aching, quiet—until you finally ask, *What did I lose that I never got to grieve?*

Ask that.

Write that.

Feel that.

Because once you name the grief, it stops pretending.

It becomes something sacred.

Something honest.

Something you can honor, release, and eventually... bless.

And in doing that, you don't just cry.

You *heal*.

9

Spiritual Travail or Depression

There's a heaviness that settles on you sometimes.
It presses on your chest, slows your steps, dims your joy.
You feel disconnected, withdrawn, fragile... maybe even hopeless.

And the world rushes to name it: *Depression.*

But what if... it's *spiritual travail?*

What if the darkness isn't your end—but your womb?

Spiritual travail is the deep, aching process your soul enters when something sacred is being born—within you, or through you. It is not a symptom. It's an *initiation.* A call to carry something not yet seen. But the carrying is exhausting. Lonely. Mysterious.

And yes—painful.

The challenge is that spiritual travail *looks* a lot like depression.

But their origins—and outcomes—are not the same.

Depression often comes from depletion: too much output, not enough return. From emotional weight your body and mind can no longer carry.

Spiritual travail, on the other hand, comes from *alignment*—and the cost of it. It comes when your soul is asked to intercede, purge, transition, ascend, or mourn what others can't even name.

So how do you tell the difference?
Ask yourself:

- Is this sadness connected to a tangible depletion—or a mysterious burden I can't explain?
- Do I feel forgotten—or *called*, but unclear why?
- Am I withdrawing from life—or being pulled inward for something divine?
- Am I dying—or transforming?

Spiritual travail may feel like depression because both involve weeping, isolation, and stillness. But depression seeks to *shut you down*, while travail seeks to *break you open*.

In travail, you may feel stripped of clarity, appetite, even motivation—but underneath it, something is rumbling. A knowing. A deep sensitivity. A spiritual alertness that doesn't make sense to the rational mind.

Travail is how prophets cried.
How mothers interceded.
How those who are spiritually tuned begin to feel the labor pains of a world about to shift—or a soul being reshaped.

This doesn't mean you shouldn't seek help. You should.
Mental health is real. Medical treatment is valid.
But don't let the world convince you that every deep ache is a disorder.
Some are *divine assignments* your mind can't interpret, but your spirit understands.

So ask God, ask your higher self, ask the silence:
Is this depression—or am I travailing?
Is something wrong—or is something holy being born?
And if the answer is travail, breathe.
Let the tears fall.
Rest between the contractions.
Trust the process of what your soul is midwifing.

Because not every breakdown is a sign you're falling apart. Some are signs you're breaking through.

10

You Don't Know You're
Crying For You

You thought the tears were about them.
The betrayal.
The breakup.
The distance.
The way they changed, or failed to show up, or never saw you clearly in the first place.

You cried over conversations that didn't go how you hoped.
Over people who didn't love you the way you needed.
Over the life you thought you'd be living by now.

But then one day, in the quiet between sobs, something clicked.
You weren't just crying for the loss.
You weren't just crying for the memory.
You were crying... *for you.*

For the version of you who kept sacrificing and calling it love.
For the one who kept quiet to keep the peace.
For the younger you who had to be strong too soon.
For the present you who always comes last, even in your own story.

The tears weren't about what someone else did.

They were about what you had to *endure* just to feel chosen, heard, safe, or valued.

You didn't know that you were the one bleeding behind the scenes of every situation you held together.

You didn't know that your tears were a homecoming.

A long-overdue reunion with the self you abandoned while trying to survive.

You may have shown up for others, supported them, healed them, prayed for them—but who showed up for you?

Who stayed when you were the one unraveling?

Who loved you without condition or cost?

And more importantly... *did you?*

There comes a moment in every soul's journey where the crying turns inward.

Not in shame. Not in regret. But in *recognition*.

You see yourself.

You hold yourself.

And you realize: I've been mourning the absence of the love I never gave *me*.

This is not to blame you. It's to free you.

Because now you know:

You are the one who's been waiting.

You are the one who deserves softness.

You are the one your tears have been calling back home.

So cry. But this time, let the cry be an embrace.

A sacred apology to your own spirit.

A promise that from here on, you will no longer abandon yourself for anyone or anything.

You will listen when you ache.

You will pause when you're tired.

You will stop shrinking to make room for others.

Because you didn't know the tears were for you.

But now you do.

And now... *you can begin to heal the one who needed you most.*

The Cleansing Cry

There are tears that burn.
Tears that ache.
Tears that leave you heavy, puffy-eyed, and exhausted.
And then...
There are tears that cleanse.
These tears don't come with screaming.
They don't need an audience.
They flow like warm rain—steady, quiet, deep.
And when they finish, you feel *different*.
Not fixed.
Not full.
But lighter.
Something got released.
Something old.
Something stuck.
Something you didn't even know was weighing you down until it left.
The cleansing cry doesn't always have a backstory.
You might just feel the buildup... and then the release.
Like a storm passing through you.
Like your body knew the timing, even if your mind didn't.

And in the aftermath, there's stillness.

A rare kind.

Not silence out of numbness—but *peace*.

An exhale. A space cleared.

A moment where you feel like your spirit just did laundry, and now you're wearing clean emotional clothes.

These tears are sacred.

They don't ask for closure, revenge, or validation.

They simply cleanse.

They prepare the ground for something new.

You may find that after this kind of cry, you don't need to talk about it.

You don't need to explain yourself.

You just feel *done*.

Not in the sense of giving up—but in the sense of *laying something down.*

And maybe that's what healing is.

Not always a grand revelation.

But a moment when you stop fighting the thing inside you, and simply let it be felt... and then released.

The cleansing cry is the soul's reset button.

It brings clarity without words.

Stillness without effort.

A softness you forgot you could feel.

If you've had one, you know it.

And if you haven't yet, trust—

When it comes, you'll recognize it.

Because afterward, you won't just feel like you cried.

You'll feel like you *let go.*

And in that space, a new you quietly rises—gentler, clearer, and ready to breathe again.

12

When Crying Is The Shift

You thought it was the end.
When your knees buckled.
When the sobs wracked your body.
When your chest felt hollow and your voice couldn't find the strength to ask for help.

You called it a breakdown.
And it was.
But not in the way the world defines it.

It wasn't the collapse of who you are—it was the *release* of who you no longer needed to be.
It wasn't weakness—it was transition.
It wasn't the end—it was the *shift*.

Sometimes, crying *is* the shift.
Not the aftermath. Not the symptom. Not the side effect.
But the moment your body, soul, and spirit agree to *change shape.*

Tears are often the sound of a soul recalibrating.
You don't always know what's shifting in the middle of the breakdown.
You just know you can't keep pretending.
Can't keep carrying.
Can't keep silencing the weight inside you.

That's when the cry comes.

And when it does—it cracks open something old.

A belief. A role. A false identity. A lie you were taught about love, worth, or who you had to be.

Crying peels it back.

Tears push it through.

And what's left afterward isn't just a clean face—it's *new space.*

This is how portals work in the spirit.

They rarely arrive as flashes of light.

They come in moments of surrender.

Moments when you can't perform strength anymore.

Moments when you finally stop holding the wall up and let it fall.

That fall? That weeping? That exhale between sobs?

That *is* the breakthrough.

That is when grace rushes in.

That is when clarity has room to speak.

You won't always feel the shift instantly.

But you'll notice a quiet difference the next day.

You'll say no a little sooner.

You'll feel less tied to proving your worth.

You'll move through the world just a touch more grounded, more honest, more *you.*

And that's how it begins.

Breakdowns become breakthroughs when you stop resisting the cry.

When you let the wave carry you into the version of you that's been waiting.

So the next time the tears come unexpectedly, fiercely, and without pause—

Don't panic.

Don't push them away.

Let them shift you.

Because sometimes, the biggest growth doesn't come with a plan—
It comes with a *cry*.

13

⁂

Crying As An Ancestral Echo

Some tears don't belong to this lifetime.
They rise from a depth you can't trace.
They come suddenly, tied to no recent memory, no present trigger—just a wave that knocks you under.

You wipe your face and ask, *Where did that come from?*

And sometimes, the answer is:
Your bloodline.

Your body is more than muscle and bone—it's a carrier of memory. And not just yours.

You hold the laughter, grief, silence, and stories of those who came before you.

Their heartbreaks.

Their sacrifices.

Their stifled screams.

Their deferred dreams.

Some ancestors never had the space to cry.

They were too busy surviving.

They swallowed their sorrow, buried their heartbreak beneath work, worship, or war.

They held it in because they had to.

And now, it moves through *you*—the one sensitive enough, present enough, awakened enough to feel it.

You may be crying over abandonment that didn't begin with you. You may be grieving losses that were passed down like heirlooms. You may feel heartache in places your own life hasn't touched—but your lineage has.

This isn't a burden—it's an *invitation*.

To witness.

To honor.

To release what could not be released before.

You are not just crying for yourself.

You are crying for your grandmother who had no one to talk to. For the father who couldn't show emotion without being shamed. For the women who mothered without ever being mothered. For the men who broke under pressure but could never fall apart.

Your tears are ancestral medicine.

You're breaking cycles not just through action, but through *emotion*—by feeling what was once forbidden.

This is not just healing.

It's redemption.

It's spiritual reparation.

It's letting your lineage know: *We no longer have to carry this pain in silence.*

When you cry and feel a heaviness lift—not just in you, but in the room, in the air, in your dreams—you've touched something sacred.

So the next time the sobs come from nowhere, pause and ask:

Whose pain am I releasing right now?

Who didn't get to cry when they needed to?

What story wants to be freed through me?

And then say, even if only in your spirit:

I see you. I feel you. I release this for us.

Because sometimes, your tears are not just your own.

They are echoes—carrying closure back through time.

14

Emotional Labor, Unpaid

You keep showing up.
Even when you're exhausted.
Even when your name isn't mentioned in the thank-yous.
Even when your love is treated like a resource, not a relationship.

You're the one they come to.
The strong one.
The dependable one.
The "you got a minute?"
The "can you just...?"
The default caretaker.

And you keep giving—because somewhere along the way, you were taught that giving is what makes you good. That overextending is what proves you love them. That being tired is normal. That being empty is *holy*.

But eventually, the body rebels.
The heart leaks.
The soul says, *No more.*

And that's when the tears come.

Not just because you're sad—but because you're *spent*.
Because you gave pieces of yourself until you forgot what wholeness felt like.

Because you smiled when you wanted to scream.

Because you poured out comfort you were never poured back.

This is emotional labor.

Unseen.

Unaccounted.

Unpaid.

The kind of labor that makes your spirit ache in places therapy can name—but only rest can heal.

And what are the wages?

Tears.

Resentment.

Feeling invisible.

Moments when you wonder, *If I stopped giving, who would notice?*

You weren't meant to be everyone's emotional backbone.

You weren't meant to be the one who carries the weight of every conflict, every apology never given, every role no one else will step into.

You became the glue—but now you're cracking.

This chapter is your permission to stop.

To renegotiate your worth.

To stop proving your value through burnout.

To recognize that love without reciprocity becomes labor.

And labor without honor becomes grief.

Your tears are not just frustration. They are invoices.

Unsent receipts for all the moments you showed up with no thanks, no space, no care.

But now—send them.

Send them to yourself.

Write the names of the people you carry.

Write the roles you never asked for.

Write the weight. And then release it.

Because your tears deserve rest.

Your love deserves return.

And your soul deserves to be seen as more than what you do for others.

Let this cry be the first step in reclaiming your balance.

Not because you don't care.

But because *you do.*

And it's time to care for the one who's done the most giving: *you.*

15

Nobody Asks If You're Okay

You answer the phone when they call.
You show up when they need you.
You remember the dates, offer the advice, hold the space, solve the problem.

But when you go quiet...

When your energy dips...

When the tears start showing in the corners of your eyes instead of your voice—

No one asks.

They assume you're fine.

They assume you're always fine.

Because you're the strong one.

And strength, in their eyes, has no off switch.

It's a strange kind of isolation, being the person everyone leans on, while quietly drowning yourself.

You start to feel the weight of being dependable, not because you're strong, but because *they never learned how to be there for you.*

You realize you've become everyone's support system—*except your own.*

And after a while, that absence of care? That silence?

It starts to grow into something sharp.

Resentment.

Not because you're selfish.

But because you're tired.

And because somewhere deep down, you hoped someone would notice your heaviness before you had to say a word.

But they didn't.

Or couldn't.

Or wouldn't.

And that hurts.

Not just because of what wasn't said—but because of what that silence revealed:

That your strength has been mistaken for invincibility.

That your giving has become expectation.

That your pain doesn't provoke concern—it provokes distance.

And yet, you still show up.

Still hold space.

Still offer grace.

But something shifts.

You start to see how unbalanced the table has become.

How few seats are set for *you.*

And it's okay to be mad about that.

It's okay to mourn the support you never got.

It's okay to let the tears fall—not just from sadness, but from the sacred rage of being unseen in your own storm.

Your strength has been a gift.

But you are allowed to outgrow the role of emotional anchor.

You are allowed to say, *I need someone to check on me, too.*

And if they don't?

Then let *you* be the one to ask:

Hey, are you okay?

Say it to the mirror.

Say it to your heart.

Say it with tenderness and truth.

Because that strong one inside of you is still human.
Still soft.
Still needing a place to land.

Let that place be *you*, if no one else knows how.

16

⌘

What Happens When You Stop Crying

There comes a moment when the tears run dry.
Not because everything is healed—
But because something within you has shifted.

You stop crying, and at first, the silence is eerie.
Still.
Too still.
You wait for the next wave. But it doesn't come.

So you ask yourself: *Is it over?*
But "over" is a layered thing.

Sometimes, when the crying stops, what follows is **numbness**.
An emotional quiet that isn't peace—it's just pause.
You're not sad anymore, but you're not joyful either.
You feel empty. Disconnected. Distant from yourself and others.

This is your soul's way of catching its breath.
After an emotional flood, numbness can be the body's temporary shelter.
Not a failure—but a survival response.

Other times, when the crying stops, what emerges is **clarity**.
Not dramatic. Not loud.

Just a knowing.

A realization.

A subtle awareness that what was weighing you down no longer holds the same power.

You see the situation, the person, or yourself differently now.

Not through the lens of pain, but through the lens of *wisdom*.

And then, sometimes, what follows is **readiness**.

Not for revenge. Not for reconciliation.

Just readiness.

To move.

To choose differently.

To live lighter.

To no longer carry what is not yours.

When you stop crying, it doesn't always mean you're healed.

But it might mean the chapter of *feeling everything all at once* has ended.

It might mean your nervous system is exhaling.

That your heart is choosing stillness over spiraling.

That your spirit is closing the wound with a slow, holy stitch.

And even if the world doesn't notice the shift, *you* will.

You'll find yourself no longer reaching out to the same person.

You'll notice your breath doesn't catch when their name is mentioned.

You'll feel space where there used to be ache.

And that's when you know—

The crying wasn't in vain.

It carried you through something.

It moved the grief.

It changed your center.

So when the tears stop, don't panic.

Don't rush to feel "normal."

Just *listen*.

Is this numbness that needs patience?

Is this clarity that needs reflection?

Is this readiness that needs your next move?

Because stopping doesn't mean abandoning the process. It means the water has done its work.

Now... what will you do with the space it left behind?

17

The First Smile After The Last Cry

You don't plan it.
You're not even expecting it.
But one day—while making tea, folding clothes, or hearing a song you forgot you loved—
You smile.

And for a moment, you pause.
Because it feels... unfamiliar.
Foreign, even.
Like something returning home after being away too long.

You didn't force it.
It just rose—quietly, sweetly, like morning sun through half-closed blinds.

Joy.
Not the loud, jump-up-and-down kind.
Not the kind that demands attention.
But a *soft joy*—the kind that tiptoes back in after sorrow has had its say.

This is the smile that comes after the weeping.

The laughter that returns when you thought you forgot how.

The warmth in your chest where heaviness used to live.

You realize that somewhere between the tears and the silence, something began to grow.

Not because the pain disappeared, but because *you endured it.*

Joy, real joy, doesn't come *instead* of sorrow—it comes *through* it.

It comes when you've honored your feelings, not bypassed them.

When you've sat in the dark long enough to recognize the light again.

The first smile after the last cry is not performative.

It's not for Instagram.

It's not to convince anyone you've "moved on."

It's just... yours.

It's the body remembering how it feels to feel *light.*

It's your nervous system releasing permission for happiness to exist again.

And maybe it shows up in a laugh you didn't expect.

Or a moment of gratitude while walking alone.

Or a breath so full, it surprises you that nothing aches in that second.

This smile is sacred.

Because it was earned.

Because it didn't erase your grief—it *rose with it.*

You'll notice, too, that you start smiling more often.

Not all the time.

Not every day.

But enough to know you're healing.

And eventually, that smile will become part of your rhythm.

Not because everything is perfect, but because *you've made peace with what isn't.*

So when it comes—don't dismiss it.

Don't question it.

Don't compare it to what once was.

Just receive it.

Let that smile stretch across your soul like a sunrise, and whisper to yourself:

I made it through.

I'm still here.

And joy still knows my name.

18

Let Crying Teach You

Every tear has something to say.
But when we're overwhelmed, we don't always stop to listen.

We cry, then wipe it away.

Cry, then apologize for it.

Cry, then move on quickly—too quickly—because we're taught that tears are interruptions, not information.

But what if the cry wasn't just a release?

What if it was a *teacher*?

What if, instead of pushing through, you paused and asked:

What was that cry trying to show me?

Maybe it was a boundary you've been afraid to set.

A truth you've been holding back.

A grief you thought you had already outgrown.

Or a wound you didn't realize still had a voice.

Emotion is intelligence.

Tears are how your body speaks what your mouth won't say.

They're the water of wisdom, flowing through you to carry meaning, memory, and sometimes, revelation.

To let the cry teach you means you allow it to finish its sentence.

It might whisper, *You're exhausted.*
It might scream, *You've been too quiet for too long.*
It might ache with the words, *That hurt more than you admitted.*
   You don't have to write an essay on it.
Just listen.
Just notice what part of you trembled the most when the tears came.
Was it the child in you? The warrior in you? The woman who always
holds everyone else together?
   Let the cry be a classroom.
   Sit with your journal afterward.
Or lay in silence and breathe.
Or simply say aloud, *I'm open to the message in this.*
   Because there is always a message.
Even in confusion.
Even in sadness.
Even in the kind of cry that comes out of nowhere and leaves you
stunned.
   The cry may come to say:

- *Let go.*
- *You've changed.*
- *They're not for you.*
- *You've been too hard on yourself.*
- *Your soul is growing, and this is the stretch.*

When you let the cry teach you, the healing deepens.
Not because the pain goes away instantly, but because you learn how
to sit with it like a sacred guest.
You stop being afraid of your own emotions.
You stop rushing past your own soul.
   So next time you cry, don't just dry your face.
Ask what the water knew.

Because that cry might be your body's way of delivering a truth your spirit has been whispering for years.

And once you listen...

You'll never cry the same way again.

19

Tears That Water New Life

There's something sacred about the tears that don't just fall—they feed.

They don't just signal pain—they awaken growth.

They don't just mark the end of a chapter—they water the roots of something entirely new.

You may not have seen it at first.

You were too deep in the heartbreak, the confusion, the unraveling.

But over time—after the crying, the silence, the release—you began to notice something stirring.

A shift.

A strength.

A soft, new version of yourself rising from the same soil that once held your grief.

Those tears were not wasted.

They were *seed water*.

Because every breakdown plants something—

Insight. Compassion. Resilience. A calling.

And tears are how you water the invisible things.

The things you didn't know you were growing while you were healing.

That season of weeping?

It opened your heart in a way joy alone never could.

It deepened your empathy.

It stretched your spirit.

It stripped you of what wasn't real and reintroduced you to who you've always been beneath the pain.

You didn't just cry.

You *cleared space*.

For purpose.

For truth.

For the version of you that could now handle the weight of what's next—with grace, with awareness, with alignment.

This is how purpose is often born—not in the loud moments, but in the wet soil of suffering.

Not in the praise, but in the process.

Not when you're at your best, but when you're at your most honest.

So no, the pain didn't come to destroy you.

It came to *break the ground*.

And what's sprouting now—

Your vision, your voice, your boundaries, your capacity to hold others, your understanding of your own worth—

That's what was growing in the dark.

You were not lost.

You were planted.

And those tears?

They were the first rain.

So tend gently to the life that's coming forth now.

Nurture it with joy.

Protect it with wisdom.

Honor it with truth.

Because everything you cried through...

Was clearing the path for *this*.

20

A Different Cry

The tears still come.
Sometimes unexpectedly.
A memory, a scent, a song, or a still moment can open the well again.
But they don't scare you anymore.

Because now, you understand:
Crying doesn't mean you're broken.
It means you're *alive*.
Present. Feeling. Listening. Healing in real time.

You've stopped apologizing for your softness.
You no longer shame yourself for needing rest, silence, or solitude.
You don't rush to explain the emotion away—you let it rise, speak, and move through you.

This doesn't mean everything is fixed.
It means you've stopped hiding from your own truth.

There was a time when tears made you feel weak.
Now, they make you feel real.

You're still vulnerable—but it's not the fragile kind.
It's the *honest* kind.
The kind that comes from knowing yourself deeply enough to show up fully—even when it's messy, even when it's tender.

You're no longer afraid to be seen in your sadness.
Because you've seen the power in it.
You've felt how grief refines.
How sorrow strips.
How emotion carves space for light to pour in.
    And you've survived.
Not just the moment—but the meaning.
You've made peace with your waves.
You've learned how to ride them instead of drown in them.
    Now, you carry your emotions with reverence.
Like sacred messengers.
Like rivers flowing through your humanity and back into your divinity.
    You're not done crying.
You don't need to be.
Because now, you cry with *awareness*.
Now, your tears aren't just a signal of overwhelm—they're part of your alchemy.
    They say: *I'm present.*
They say: *I'm growing.*
They say: *I feel, therefore I heal.*
    And with every tear that falls, you reclaim something that was never meant to be buried.
    So no, you're not done crying.
    But you are *different now.*
    More grounded.
More aware.
More whole.
    And when the next wave comes, you'll meet it—not with fear, but with welcome.
    Because you know what lives on the other side of tears.
    You know the language of the soul.
    And you finally trust your own ability to listen, to feel, and to *rise.*

About The Author

Wendy Hood writes and publishes awakening literature that stretches across dimensions, speaking to those who are ready to remember what they already know. Her books blend metaphysics, psychology, healing, and storytelling, often infused with intuitive codes and light frequencies. As a writer, Wendy channels clarity for theseeker, the orphaned soul, and the spiritually gifted who may not yet know their purpose.

For retail, bulk orders, workshops, or to explore more teachings:
Author & Creator: Wendy Hood
Publishing House: 2Earths Publishing Co.
Email: 2earths.publishingco@gmail.com
Website: wendyhood-books.com

www.ingramcontent.com/pod-product-compliance
Lightning Source LLC
Chambersburg PA
CBHW070945120626
46546CB00004B/1571